# *OUR LADY OF THE ORGASM*

## Nin Andrews

a plume editions book

AN IMPRINT OF MADHAT PRESS

ASHEVILLE, NORTH CAROLINA

MadHat Press
MadHat Incorporated
PO Box 8364, Asheville, NC 28814

The Library of Congress has assigned
this edition a Control Number of
2016915270

ISBN 978-1-941196-37-3 (paperback)

Cover art and design by Marc Vincenz
Book design by MadHat Press

www.MadHat-Press.com

First Printing

# TABLE OF CONTENTS

# OUR LADY OF THE ORGASM

# The orgasm thinks you have forgotten her

that you no longer feel her like a tingle, a tug, or a whispered word in the back of your mind. That you have taken from her whatever you wished, whatever you wanted, whatever you thought you must have. And you have tossed her aside without looking back.

It happened so easily, she sighs—as easily as pulling a thread from a hem, unraveling her slowly at first, then faster and faster. Now she wakes, late and alone, with a memory of all she has lost. All that once shaped the hours around her like a lit and shimmering gown.

# The orgasm wants to be famous

She thinks success would be her best revenge. It's not enough for her now, merely to be alive. Or to feel bliss in brief moments. No, she wants to be seen. Known. She wants everyone to cheer her on. Not just you. And why shouldn't they? She knows she's a very special orgasm. She can see it every time she looks at her reflection, pirouetting before the mirror and then leaping this way and that. She cannot take her eyes off of herself. She is as lovely as a star. How could so few know she exists? She imagines the world fluttering around her like insects around a lamp. The image gives her pause. She thinks again. She selects a more appealing image—perhaps they will flit around her like fireflies around the moon.

OUR LADY OF THE ORGASM

# The orgasm decides to learn about social media

because that is where fame happens these days. It is no longer satisfying simply to be an orgasm with long, silky legs. She must also exist on the web. At first she is taken in by the easy access to so many fans. But soon it makes her feel frivolous. And a bit exposed. She begins to worry that she lacks depth. Her encounters are so frequent and fleeting. She fears she is becoming the kind of orgasm who merely tickles the surface of the lake. Who never dives deep like a fish or flies high like an angel. How could she when her legs are still tucked so neatly beneath her, her wings folded neatly across her back? Outside the clouds rush past like messages from another world. And the sky turns from blue to black.

3

# The orgasm wants to open a Twitter account

but she isn't sure what to tweet. At first she follows other tweeters. They tweet and tweet, forever singing to their wonderful selves. Even when she is sleeping, they are tweeting. Even when the snow falls and cuts off her electricity. Even when she wakes the morning after, cold and shivering, and wraps herself in a robe. One day she decides to tweet, too. *I am lighting up a cigarette*, she tweets. *And I am telling you the one real truth*. She licks her lips and smiles. *I am your last orgasm*. She enjoys the silence that follows and is just about to sign off of Twitter forever. But then someone retweets her tweet. And someone else retweets the retweet. A little flutter begins in her heart. She sucks in deeply and glows like the tip of her lit cigarette.

# The orgasm decides she must become a brand

Otherwise she will be like every other aspiring orgasm—i.e., anonymous. Lost among side streets and absent minds. But how can she become unique? How can she separate herself from the others? There are so many. She thinks of them with disdain—those everyday orgasms that are so irksome, they are like used cars with their ignition problems, their lubrication issues, their broken distributors and failing circuitry. She is nothing like them. Of course she isn't. She's sleek and shiny and freshly painted. She decides she must become a niche orgasm, a brand all her own—something everyone desires but few ever possess, much less drive.

# The orgasm is building a website

but is not sure what to put on her home page. She wants to draw something to fill the empty space. She imagines past admirers and ex-lovers stopping by, wanting to know her every detail. *How is she?* they ask. *Has she aged? Has she grown fat and wrinkly and sad?* She knows they are watching her from afar, tapping her with their mind's eye. Their presence makes her shudder. Makes her want to design the page as a cemetery or design a cemetery as a page between her and the world. All it takes, she reminds herself, is a shovel and knowing what to do with the dirt. She draws a graveyard with maple trees and tombstones, an ex-lover's name on each one. She blesses them all as they once blessed her. She wishes them to rest in peace. In her mind she hears a wintry wind and the rustling of dry leaves.

# The orgasm fell in love with you once

yes, you; but it did not end well. Afterward, she dreamt of you night and day. Each time she saw you walking by, she wanted to call out, *I love you, I want you, please come back,* but the words sat silently on the windowsill as if they were merely considering the weather, as if *I love you* were a chance of cloudiness or rain, as if love might need to carry an umbrella, or perhaps wear a rain hat, a red scarf, or galoshes. Or a light coat. Yes, a light-blue *I love you* coat, hanging loosely from her freckled shoulders, unbuttoned to the wind, the cruel wind of *I love you,* as she wandered the streets below your apartment with the words *I love you* blowing through her mind, scattering her like confetti, like all the unsent love notes she composed on sleepless nights before she saw you leaving The Café Loup at dusk, and you smiled and turned to her as if at last you would acknowledge her again. When she opened her mouth to say *I love you,* the words were right there on the tip of her tongue. But when she looked and saw you again, all at once you were not the you she loved. How could she explain it? How love suddenly detached from her skin? And the wonder she felt then, the relief. She was overwhelmed by an inexplicable urge to dance.

# The orgasm remembers you, her ex

and asks the evening air, *Who are you now?* She thinks of the anguish you caused, those sleepless nights when she sobbed alone. Sometimes she had to wring out the sheets the morning after. Sometimes she howled like a dog at the moon. She texted and phoned you so often, but you never answered her calls. She is amazed at how ordinary you looked when she finally saw you in your faded skinny jeans, your tall black boots, smoke billowing from your red-red lips. That's when she asked herself, *Who were you that made me love you so much and for so long?*

She knows the answer. You were but a dream. A dream of an orgasm. But who are you now when she no longer dreams of you?

# The orgasm is not sure about the About Me page.

What can she say about herself? That she was once a cello? Well, not a cello exactly, but the notes that emerged? No, not the notes exactly, but the aura of the notes, the small ache they left in the sky like an imprint in blue—though it wasn't a sky exactly, but the cloudless space, there, opening and opening inside every woman. (She always did have a preference for women.)

# The orgasm needs a photo of herself

preferably a head shot to go with a short bio. She takes a selfie leaning against a tree, looking too posed, looking not at all *au naturel* as she'd planned. She takes another selfie sitting on the hood of her car, smiling. Behind her, written on the front window's condensation, is her message to the world. She throws them both away. Then she lets her hair cover her eyes and mouth and tries again. She doesn't want everyone to know what she looks like. No orgasm does. There is a rule against an orgasm who shows too much in public. A rule against an orgasm who shows too much in private, too. Who lets anyone gaze into her soft brown eyes.

# The orgasm reads she must offer something to her fans

if she wants people to Like her. And she does. She wants all the Likes she can get even if she doesn't actually like them back. She decides to offer a short audio course on how to like an orgasm. Just thinking of it, she feels important. She feels pity, too, for all those who have no clue how to like her. Some don't even know who she is. The orgasmless, she notes, are everywhere. Among them are queens, presidents, the Pope—all the men and women whose alarm clocks start ringing long before dawn when they rush out into the day, leaving her alone to dream in their sunlit beds.

# To the Friends of the Orgasm

There are a few things you should know. For example, you might think the orgasm should be happy to greet you, and of course she is. But the orgasm, like all orgasms, (have you noticed this?) loves to complain. Because the orgasm population is in decline. Their unemployment rate is on the rise. Soon it will be as high as 25%. In addition many suffer from feelings of alienation and abandonment and a tendency toward melancholia. *Are you ever going to adopt a more generous policy and open heart? Soul? Legs?* they ask. Some are even showing suicidal tendencies. Even as they speak or whisper your name, they try to grab a toe or lick a finger or hold you in a wistful glance. But they can't hold on for long. They are so easily distracted these days, so quick to forget. Some get lost between one thought and the next. *What did you say?* they ask. They look so downcast. So distraught. They suspect they are losing you. That you are no better than the rest. They have already begun to speak of you in the past tense.

# Against Amnesia

Everyone knows that if a tree falls in the woods, and no one hears it, it makes no sound. That if an orgasm sighs in the dark, and no one listens, the sigh is silent. If God flames among the bushes, and there is no Moses nearby, His words are like the mumblings of a madman. For the trees, like the orgasms, like the flames and God, must share their shadows, their thoughts, their loneliness in order to exist at all. If an orgasm does not dream the world and all its aspects, the world has no soul. Without a soul, there is no life or wind, no breath and no trembling or blazing leaves. This is the mathematic equation known by orgasms alone. It is their job to keep the sacred balance, to keep us all from curling inward like a scroll, never to be read or known.

# The Boy Called Joe

## I.

Throughout history there have been sightings of such supernatural being as Our Lady of the Orgasm. The sightings are rare and are one of the signs that mark a person as the kind of guru or saint who can change the very course of human history. Joe the Guru is among the few from the twentieth century to witness Our Lady of the Orgasm and was instantly converted. He was only a teenager when he first glimpsed her. He later abandoned all worldly affairs and committed himself completely to her devotion. Stories are told about his childhood in which he is fondly referred to as the Boy called Joe.

## II.

It started when he was very young. There was always a vision waiting to be seen. How could he explain it? Others never saw them—those heavenly beings who were forever eating the sugar cubes at teatime and stealing sips of his parents' martinis at cocktail parties. They winked at him conspiratorially, knowing he would never tell.

## III.

When he was fourteen, he woke one night and saw Our Lady of the Orgasm singing and was filled by notes so beautiful, he ascended with them, up and up, like bubbles in a glass of champagne before breaking into tears and falling back to earth as a shower of rain. The next day he had such a high fever, his mother placed a bag of frozen peas on his forehead. She knew he was changed. For years after, he pretended he was as ignorant as his parents who walked through their days like children in a game of pin-the-tail-on-the-donkey. But whenever he closed his eyes, he saw Our Lady again, her buttocks as round and rosy as beatified peaches.

# How to Love an Orgasm

The orgasm decides to monetize her website. To sell her advice. She needs to reach more people. After all, she wants to save the world, or at least herself. Isn't that's why she exists? Soon, she thinks, anyone will be able to click *here* for a free sample of her voice. But she's not sure what to say. Nevertheless, she begins: *I want to take this moment to thank you for purchasing* How to Love an Orgasm. *I promise that you will not be sorry. Learning how to love an orgasm is nothing short of a life-changing skill.*

She pauses. *Is love a skill?* She thinks so. But she is making this up as she goes.

*If you are driving while listening to this recordin*g, she continues, *please pull over. If you are washing dishes or ironing shirts, please put the sponge or the iron down. If you are operating any heavy machinery, please stop. You do not need any machinery in order to love an orgasm.* She shudders involuntarily and tries to suppress the memory of being turned on an off with a flick of a switch.

*Close your eyes and take a deep breath*, she says. *Feel the sun, warm on your skin. Imagine the cries of gulls overhead.*

*Now, imagine you are the gull, flapping your wings and soaring.*

She pauses. Is she wasting her time? How often has the taught her humans to fly? And to swim and breathe underwater? As soon as she leaves, they forget.

Forgetting is their greatest blessing and curse—it keeps them alive, and it keeps them crawling like ants on the ground.

# The Golden Nugget

The Golden Nugget, for those who don't know, is a little golden rocket ship that a woman can insert inside herself. Not a little inside, but all the way in, as the directions state. And the Golden Nugget will find places in a woman no man has been. It will go on tour. Or what the advertisement calls *The Golden Tour.*

*Did you know there are entire galaxies in there,* the directions claims, *complete with stars, planets and meteor showers?*

But there are warnings. After a while, some women grow afraid that they are being taken over by the Golden Nugget. *What if the Golden Nugget is some kind of alien?* one lady worries. *What if one of those space ships that landed ages ago in Roswell, New Mexico brought aliens who found a secret way to impregnate women? They packaged themselves in plastic wrap and wait on the shelves in sex shops across America. Unwitting women pop them inside, thinking they're just another dildo.* She thinks a lot of men wouldn't mind being mistaken for just another dildo, but only the aliens would figure out how to do it.

*But why worry now?* she thinks. Now when she can live her fairytale dream, gliding into the horizon, sighing with every step, and at every bird and butterfly flitting past, and every drop of unpredicted rain.

# The orgasm reads that she should email her fans directly

if she wants them to know her or purchase her work. She should remind them how much they want her. Tell them tidbits about her beautiful and delicious self. But she's a shy orgasm. She doesn't like to be too forward. Nevertheless, she begins to wonder *What would I say to my fans?* She wishes she could ask them *What do you want to hear?* Or, better yet, *What would you say if you were me?* She imagines her fans as orgasms. Some would be small and secretive like minnows swimming in the shallows. Others would come in groups like schools of fish. Still others would be sharks—the kind who give orgasms a bad name.

*Nin Andrews*

# The orgasm thinks she suffers from SAD

or seasonal affective disorder. On dark winter days, she no longer wants to be an orgasm. She no longer wants to get out of bed or shower or rush out into the evening as she has always done. She tells herself *I must rise and shine*, but doesn't budge. She can't even begin to rise, much less shine. *What is the matter with me?* she asks her reflection. She who has always been so spontaneous.

But the truth is, she is chilled to the bone. Soon, she fears, she will be frozen solid. For days she sits on the windowsill staring coldly at the sky. On sunny days, she drips. *Don't look*, her neighbors whisper. *She's crying*. But that's just how she prays. For an orgasm, prayer is similar to melting in the same way that sinning is similar to talking in your sleep.

*Let me die. Let me die one more time*, she says, her lips barely moving. The neighbors throw snowballs and shovel their sidewalks, always turning their backs to her. But one man glances her way. There's always one good Samaritan out there. He doesn't know the danger he is in.

# The orgasm thinks of writing a self-help book

or at least reading one. After all, she is in dire need of help. She no longer wants to be an orgasm. She thinks maybe she can write her way to happiness. To God. But she can't help wondering *Is there a God of orgasms?* So often men and women have called out to Him in her presence. Her friend, Joe the Guru, says there is a God of everything. She thinks about this. A God of the beetles and birds. Of wind. And nut trees. And lust. She writes *Today I saw God. He was in the air, the sunlit dust, and the sea. I felt him ripple within me.* It sounds so nice, she thinks. But she doesn't believe a word of it. Why would God be in the dust? Or water? Or worse, herself? She puts on her slippers. She imagines God putting on His slippers. Her feet feel suddenly warm. Maybe a little too warm.

# The orgasm is so depressed

she begins to cry. Softly at first, and then a full wail. How often she has said never again. Joe the Guru suspects that she's bipolar. She's afraid he's right. She's also afraid of being mortal. She's afraid of being immortal, too. *Hush!* Joe says. *Stop listening to your fears. Your fears are no more you than your gown. Try to be courageous!* That's why he took her to a healing ceremony where she tried walking on coals. She waited until the coals had cooled, then raced across. But she tripped and fell, and the hem of her skirt caught fire. She rolled on the ground until she was nothing but smoldering shame. Afterward she worried. What if the fire had spread? What if it had lit up her loose threads, traveled across the floor and leapt from windows and into the streets and the town beyond? What if she became the flaming torch that set the whole world ablaze? She can't stop thinking about this. *From now on I must live alone*, she thinks, crying herself to sleep. Her dreams turn to flames and burn pinholes in the night.

# Joe the Guru is the only one who knows the truth

i.e., that she is unique among orgasms. For she is as different from other members of her tribe as water from sand, as honey from Tabasco sauce. Indeed, he should know. It is she who saved him from being a dormant bud of a man. It happened on an ordinary evening when he was still a teenager, smoking his first joint. Just as he was drifting off, he had a vision in which he saw her in all her radiance, quivering and singing and fluttering with the angels. She, he learned, is none other than Our Lady of the Orgasm. In heaven, statuettes of her are placed on altars and dangle from the rearview mirrors of cars. Angels are known to rub her for good luck before flying to the depths below. But alas, he realized, she has forgotten her divine nature, as men and orgasms are wont to do.

# Joe the Guru instructs the orgasm

that she must discover her true purpose in life. Only then, he says, will she find her soul again. And be happy. But she has never had a purpose. That much she feels certain she knows. Instead she has always imagined herself as a kind of poetry. Or music. *But what's the use of that?* Joe asks. *Nothing*, she sighs, adding, *Not everything is utilitarian, Joe.* In spite of herself she remembers a lover who called her *my favorite soporific.* How loudly he snored. Sometimes, when she couldn't stand it, she nibbled the tender skin behind his ear, inside his elbow, or at the curve of his leg. And if that didn't work, she bit gently into the tip of his penis until he woke with a yelp. *I had such a nightmare*, he would say. *A rat was gnawing on me as if I were a piece of cheese.* She never told a soul about this. But surely she's more than an aid for sleep.

# Sometimes the orgasm thinks Joe the Guru might be mistaken

or even delusional—the way he is forever singing her praises, raving not only about her lips and freckles and dimples but also about the puffy clouds in the sky, the lime-green caterpillars eating the zinnias, *those future butterflies* he calls them, as if they were metaphors for her. Is he a guru or a lunatic? she wonders. Is she the one who needs help or is he? She thinks of how he is forever comforting her, wiping away her tears and combing her hair until it shines. Sometimes it gives off sparks and rises in an angry, electric halo. Then she floats up with it, first five feet, then ten. How pathetic he looks beneath her, fluttering his pale fingers, trying to grab hold of her, as if she were a hat caught by a sudden wind.

# The orgasm decides to become a poet

and signs up for a class at a community college. She is happy to see that they accept all kinds at the college. She doesn't feel a bit out place. But her professor is forever berating the aspiring poets. *This is not a poem!* he tells the class *You lack discipline. You lack form and style. Have you never read the classics?* The orgasm is reminded of her early days of learning how to be an orgasm. Often she heard, *That's not an orgasm. Haven't you done your homework?*

There were so many tests back then, difficult tests. Walking through walls, for example. For real orgasms, everyone knows, there is no such thing as a wall. Nothing stops them. At first she bumped into every wall she met, her skin a purple bruise. No matter how great her pain, she kept trying until she walked through wall after wall like a regular Houdini of orgasms. That's when she discovered that when the walls moved through her, especially the stone ones, she caught a chill. Her temperature dropped twenty degrees, and she started to sneeze. *It's like this*, she learned, *whenever you make love to the ones with no hearts or souls.* She had only meant to walk through the walls, not love them. It was the same way with the poems. She had to be careful which ones would travel inside her. And which she must never compose.

# The orgasm writes a letter to her fans

*Dear Friends, Fans, and Lovers of the Orgasm, I thought you should know more about me,* she begins. *I know you want to. Now is your chance.* She blushes even as she writes. She sounds like an advertisement. She begins again: *Dear Friends and Fans, I wanted to tell you a secret. A secret I have told no one. I miss you. I miss you as much as you miss me.*

But what if they haven't missed her? What if they don't even like her? And why should they? She isn't exactly faithful. Or easy, is she? What with her spasmodic moans and gasps, her heroic little dances and sudden professions of love. And afterward, what's left? Apologies, tears, regret? Imprints of her teeth on tender skin? It's true, the rumors that suggest she sometimes mistakes a lover for a loaf of freshly baked bread.

# Write about yourself

the writing professor tells the orgasm. But who is that? The orgasm has no clue. The professor suggests she familiarize herself with the dictionaries, and she does. She opens first the dictionary of English Orgasms, then the French. She prefers the French, of course. *Don't we all?* she asks. Just looking at a word like *fenêtre*, she enters its moonlit windows and attic rooms, then curls up inside and purrs like a cat. She doesn't even bother with the German orgasms—she has heard rumors that they are the ones who mistake the orgasm for a sneeze. Or is it vice versa? She's not sure. But she does want to make distinctions. She is an orgasm with some taste.

But then she decides it doesn't really matter who she is. After all, the others in the class are simply describing their past, as if that defines them. So she describes the emptiness of her own childhood. The long pale days in a remote town where even the schoolhouse had hollow rooms and classes full of hours that would never end. The orgasm was so small. No one noticed her or commented on her tiny pink hands. It was then that she began to long for something else. Anything else. And her longing grew. It made her ache and burn, traveling up and down the hairs on her legs like a flame. Until one day she shone like a small sun. Others began to look at her then. They sought her company again and again. Some thought of her as the only recess they ever had.

# The orgasm wants to write a memoir

but she doesn't know how to begin. When she thinks of the early days, she remembers how everyone warned her. *You'll never succeed. Many try to be orgasms and fail.* But she knew she was different. In secret, she practiced. She told no one about this, not even her cat—and yes, all orgasms keep cats, which is why cats have little need of company. She began slowly, gathering her nerve. She only had one nerve, and it took everything she had to gather it up. Sometimes she gathered it for weeks at a time, starting at the ceiling, first climbing down the walls, and then back up again, clinging for hours to the chandelier. Then, all at once, she fell, twisting and turning in the air. She fell many times. Each time she rose again, a part of her became atoms of light, swirling up toward the sky. *This!* she thought each time. *This is it!* But it never was. Not for long. There never was an it.

# The Six Realms of the Orgasm

after Claire Bateman

The orgasm describes the five realms she had to travel through to arrive where she is today. How, in the first realm of the orgasm, a vote was taken to see which humans are allowed to have an orgasm. And which orgasms were licensed to own a human.

In the second realm of the orgasm, also known as the suburbs, young and aspiring orgasms were welcomed as long as they remained silent and offered only controlled doses of euphoria.

In the third realm of the orgasm, also known as the business district, orgasms were tracked, counted, and rated for their annual performances. In this realm orgasms were expected to attain bliss at least three times a week, and they had to be earned, not freely given.

In the fourth realm, also known as the government offices, orgasms took balletic leaps into the dark. What happened next is classified information.

In the fifth realm, also known as the Vatican, orgasms called out to God and moaned about the fleeting nature of their existence. Some sought newer and younger humans to ward off feelings of mortality despite the general consensus that such actions are sinful and reflect a profound lack of faith.

In the sixth realm, or the afterlife, the orgasm is said to wake to discover one of three things: a) it has been reincarnated; (b) it is but a ghost or a memory of yesterday's orgasm; or (c) it is with the angels now, setting the sky on fire.

Some, it is said, never attain the sixth level but instead grow fainter and fainter until their dim light can not be detected, and even their dreams have faded from deep blue to gray to a pale and smoky white.

# Our Lady of the Orgasm

On special occasions including wedding showers, Junior League luncheons and garden-club parties, the orgasm manifests as Our Lady of the Orgasm and offers lessons on orgasm perfection and selection, complete with PowerPoints that illustrate the precise ratio of flesh size to orgasm, the slogan on every slide: *Your perfect orgasm awaits you now!* She explains how to read the size chart, the pyramid of black boxes moving from small to large, from sizes A to D, the weights and heights, 4 feet to 6, 80 pounds to 240 and beyond. She doesn't mention the plus-size orgasms, but if someone asks, she says it is best to start small. Then she adds that sadly, few ladies know how to properly unravel their minds and bodies and let the orgasm envelop them. She places a net on one hand, as if to demonstrate the orgasm's need to encircle a lady and then sink all the way into each gully and rivulet and fold. The audience inhales quickly as the heat rises in the room.

# The orgasm thinks of writing a spiritual treatise

but then she remembers how she used to be a follower of Joe the Guru who was forever quoting Joseph Campbell: *follow your bliss*. In those days bliss was all she wanted. Bliss and more bliss. Bliss, she thought, was God. She tries not to dwell on bliss these days. She's too old and tired now. But she feels a flash of pleasure just thinking of the word. A small flash, to be sure, but it triggers three other feelings. An *if only* feeling. An *ahhhh* feeling like a wish she can't fulfill. And greed. She is so sick of greed. In spite of herself, she begins to whine, *Please? Oh please?* Her *please* sends pangs of longing through her veins, opening her like a door she cannot shut. *Is there no help for an aging orgasm?* she asks. When she's open like that, who knows who will come in? The morning after, she will sigh *Look what the cat brought in.* She always blames the cat.

# The orgasm wants to write her own obituary

but she doesn't know how she will die. Each time she thinks, *This is it*, she comes back to life. Nevertheless, she begins to write: *I will die on a rainy Friday in Poland, Ohio. I remember it already. The cat would not leave my side.* Then she stops and wonders. What if it happens on a sunny day? In Paris? So she writes, *I will die on a sunny day in Paris, Texas. I remember it exactly because you brought me a single pink rose. But you did not cry.* She pauses and puts down her pen. *No*, she thinks, and she is suddenly certain. It will happen on snowy day. A Tuesday in Sorrento. She writes, *I will die on a snowy Tuesday in Sorrento, Maine. I remember how you called to me, softly, and your words became soft gray clouds blowing out to sea.* But what if she's wrong?

Exasperated, she kneels down and begins to pray to St. Teresa, the patron saint of orgasms. St. Teresa who said death is better than life. Of course, she was right. The orgasm saw a painting of St. Teresa in *The Oxford Encyclopedia of Angels, Orgasms, and Saints*. In the picture a male angel was plunging an arrow deep inside the saint's heart. Her mouth was open in an expression of anguished ecstasy. The orgasm stared at the painting for a long time, thinking a little ecstasy is still nice now and again, but she's not so sure about that arrow in the heart. She tries again to imagine a perfect death. Or maybe just a perfect metaphor for death. She often compares herself to a cigarette. Someone lighting her up and inhaling deeply while she quivers and burns. And turns to smoke. A pile of ash. In the end, there are no witnesses. Except the cat. A single rose on the sill. And two gray clouds vanishing into the sea.

# The orgasm seeks her *raison d'être*

If she just knew her *raison d'être*, the orgasm reads in *Spiritual Advice for Orgasms*, then she would know who she really is. And her life would be so much easier. So she gives herself homework. Every day she must write a statement describing who she is or isn't. Who all orgasms are and aren't. It sounds simple enough. But she can never begin. Every morning she stares at the blank page, her mind as foggy as a rainy day in Paris.

One morning she decides instead to define all the orgasms she knows, starting with the French orgasms, the ones she loves best. She will compare and contrast these orgasms, and see if she can see herself in their midst, or in their cathedrals and bistros and their perfumeries where they are forever spritzing their hair with eau de cologne or putting a dab of scent on their wrists or their pale swan necks.

The art of defining and comparing one orgasm to another, she discovers, is not a respectable task. It is, at best, a way of treating orgasms as toys, as something the cat dragged in and left on the doormat, half-dead.

# The Difference between One Orgasm and Another

1. The difference between a real orgasm and a potential orgasm is like the difference between nonfiction and fiction, the orgasm explains,

which is like the difference between hash browns and crème brulée. While you might at first glance think they are very different, hash browns and crème brulée are both edible, both yellow and white and tan, and both rich in fat, starch, and flavor. Nevertheless, one wouldn't want to be served one when ordering the other.

2. The difference between a sleeping orgasm and a fantasy orgasm is like the difference between nonfiction and creative nonfiction,

which is like the difference between night and day. While you might think that they are opposites, both are mere times of the day. While some enjoy the lit hours, others prefer not to wear sunglasses or a hat just to step outside, and are terrified of being burned by the sun's dangerous rays. And of course, both are unavoidable experiences in the course of even the most humdrum of daily lives.

3. The difference between a theoretical orgasm and an angelic orgasm is like the difference between flash fiction and prose poetry,

which is much like the difference between the dead and the living. While such a difference might seem drastic; one might assume that one kind is absent, and the other present, that is not necessarily the case. Some people believe they experience death in life (or many little deaths), while others believe there is a better life after death that begins the instant they are free to fly away from the bonds of earthly existence.

4. The difference between a female orgasm and a fake orgasm is like the difference between free verse and formal poetry,

which is like the difference between salt and pepper. While at first taste, they seem quite different, they are both mere condiments on the dining room table. And while one is deemed healthful and can be used in excess, assuming one can take the heat, the other makes a wonderful preservative and has been valued throughout the ages by men and women around the globe. For ideal relationships, one should consider ample use of both.

# A Glossary of French Orgasms

Averse, *nf*
A sudden shower of orgasms. Also, a deluge of pleasure.

Bougonnement, *nm*
A grumpy orgasm. An orgasm that is always complaining, *Is that the best you can do?*

Croissé, *nf*
An orgasm that takes you to the place where life and death part, where heaven and earth meet.

Diablesse, *nf*
An orgasm that burns, or at least singes your skin.

Étoile, *nf*
An orgasm that thinks it is the only star in your heaven.

Fraude, *nf*
A fake or deceptive orgasm. Also, a smuggler of orgasms.

Gifle, *nm*
An orgasm that slaps you in the face. Also, a wakeup call.

Hargne, *nf*
An ill-tempered orgasm that makes you pay for your sins, or at least confess them.

Idem, *nf*
An orgasm that is always the same. A regular, everyday orgasm.

Jouet, *nm*
An orgasm that treats you like a toy, or something to play with when she's bored. Also, the orgasm next door.

Kamikaze, *nm*
An orgasm that can only happen once in a lifetime. Also, a lethal orgasm.

Local, *nm*
An orgasm from your hometown. Also, an orgasm with pompoms.

Moulant, *nm*
An orgasm that fits you as snugly as a wool dress, hot out of the dryer.

Narratrice, *nf*
An orgasm that narrates events as they happen.

Ombre, *nf*
A shadowy orgasm who takes your light away forever.

Prisme, *nm*
A transcendental orgasm. An orgasm that changes the way you see the world.

Quotepart, *nf*
The number of orgasms you are allowed to have in a single life.

Rappel, *nm*
An orgasm that cries out again and again. Also, an orgasm that reminds you of its speed.

Spectateur, -trice, *n*
An orgasm that watches you, as if from above, whenever it makes love to you. Also, an out-of-body orgasm.

Tragique, *nm*
An orgasm that ends badly. An orgasm that regrets having met you.

Utopie, *nf*
The afterlife of the orgasm. And the afterlife of the afterlife of the orgasm.

Vague, *nf*
An orgasm wave. Also, an orgasm that washes over you not once, but at least three times before leaving.

Watt, *nm*
A unit of power, used to measure the current flowing through the heart of the orgasm.

Xénophobe, *nf*
An orgasm that dislikes anything new. A conservative orgasm.

Yoyo, *nm*
An orgasm that changes its mind frequently. Also, an orgasm on a string.

Zeste, *nm*
The peel of an orgasm. The flavor or spirit of the thing. Also, a tiny orgasm with a large bang.

# ACKNOWLEDGMENTS

Many thanks to the following journals who published some of the poems in this book.

*Barn Owl Review*
*The Best American Poetry Blog*
*Coconut*
*Exit 7*
*Five Points*
*Harpur Palate*
*PoetsArtists*
*Plume*
*Scapegoat*

Also, special thanks to Siena Oristaglio, Noah Blumenson-Cook, and Karina Vahitova of the Void Academy who did their best to teach me about social media and my web presence, and who helped to inspire this book. And many thanks to my poet-friends, Rick Bursky, Sammy Greenspan, Karen Schubert, Shivani Mehta, and Kathleen McGookey for their encouragement and editorial assistance. And a thousand thanks to my beloved Jim who sees the world through the eyes of a scientist but supports my ongoing quests for poetry and enlightenment in whatever forms they might take.

# ABOUT THE AUTHOR

**NIN ANDREWS** received her BA from Hamilton College and her MFA from Vermont College. The recipient of two Ohio Arts Council grants, she is the author of seven chapbooks and seven full-length collections of poetry. She also edited *Someone Wants to Steal My Name*, a book of translations of the French poet, Henri Michaux. Her most recent book, *Why God Is a Woman*, won the Ohioan Award for Poetry in 2016.

www.ingramcontent.com/pod-product-compliance
Lightning Source LLC
Chambersburg PA
CBHW031542040426
42445CB00010B/656